Debt Elimination

The Ultimate Guide to

Financial Prosperity

by

I0474227

J. P. Conyers, Jr.

PUBLISHED BY:
James P. Conyers Jr.
Copyright © 2012

Disclaimer

Disclaimer and Terms of Use: No information contained in this book should be considered as physical, health related, financial, tax, or legal advice.

Your reliance upon information and content obtained by you at or through this publication is solely at your own risk. The author assumes no liability or responsibly for damage or injury to you, other persons, or property arising from any use of any product, information, idea, or instruction contained in the content provided to you through this book.

The individuals and situations in this book may or may not be real. The characters and situations in this book are used to deliver certain points and are for example purpose only.

4

Legal Notice

We have used our best efforts in preparing this book and the accompanying materials.

We make no representation or warranties with respect to the accuracy, applicability, fitness, or completeness of the contents of this book. The information contained in this book is strictly for informational purposes.

This book doesn't come with any warranties (express or implied), merchantability, or fitness for any particular purpose. We shall in no event be held liable to any party for any direct, indirect, punitive, special, incidental or other consequential damages arising directly or indirectly from any use of this material, which is provided "as is", and without warranties.

Dedication

I would like to dedicate this book to all the people that are in debt, hurting, and stressed beyond belief. I know how you feel because I was once in your position.

I'm here to tell you, you can get out of debt and own your life but you must decide to make some changes. You have to want to get out of debt and change a few behaviors that got you into the debt you current have.

Statistics show that around 90% - 95% of the population lives in debt. They also show that only a small percentage of people, around 5% - 10% live a truly debt free lifestyle.

If you will apply the simple techniques outlined in this book you should be able to have similar results in becoming debt free in only a handful of years.

I am a person with integrity and want you to know up front that the techniques are simple to implement but it will take constant desire and determination to stick with them until the debt is eliminated.

I'm here to tell you, you can do it! You just have to become dedicated and have a stick to it attitude. In just a few short years you will own your life and can be one of the top 10% of the people that are financially free.

Imagine in only a few years taking a cruise and paying cash, building your child's education fund, saving for retirement, building wealth, etc.

Dream big and make getting out of debt fun and before you know it you'll be living a totally different, stress free lifestyle.

What is your plan for your future, one that you control or one the banks and credit card companies control?

Are you going to be one of the 10% financially free individuals that choose where, when and how they enjoy their lives? Or are you going to be one that is stressed out when you retire, with bills piling up, or having to work two jobs until you pass away.

You see one of the above statistics is going to fit your life. It's going to be one or the other.

You are in control and you are the ultimate decision makers. For every day you delay getting out of debt you are losing a lifetime of wealth.

I hope you choose to be smart and start reducing your debt today. I'm sure you will be glad you did, especially when you are able to pay that last debt off.

Here's to your success and remember!

"You can finance for your child's education, but you cannot finance for your retirement."
Unknown Author

Table of Contents

Foreword

I would first like to thank you for your purchase. It is your first step in achieving a debt-free lifestyle. In this book you will discover the techniques necessary for you to take your life back from debt.

Now that we have determined that you are serious about conquering debt and have taken that hard first step by purchasing this book, I want to assure you that if you take action and consistently apply the techniques in this book you will achieve a debt-free lifestyle and start to build true wealth.

Truly we all would love to be debt-free, but only a small few of the overall population ever seem to achieve it.

One of the most important ingredients for you to make this system work is to consistently applying these techniques.

Most people can fully achieve a debt-free life within a handful of years. Each person's situation is different and it will depend on the varying amount of debt to be repaid.

It's very important for you to be accountable for your new destiny and I want you to remember when it gets hard for you, there is an end in sight. You will only reach your goal of debt-free living by consistently applying these techniques.

I have faith in you and know that the other option of retiring dead broke, or working through retirement for the rest of your life, is not a life I want to live.

From this point on it is your choice. A choice you will have to live with for the rest of your life. Some individuals get a feeling they will pay their debt off somewhere down the road. I'm sorry to say statistics show that day rarely comes. That's why 90% -95% of individuals retire broke, leaving only 5% - 10% financially independent by the age of 65.

Are you going to depend on the Government for your retirement? What quality of life do you want? Are you going to travel later in life, go on a dream vacation? Provide your kids or grandkids with a college education?

If you don't take action to correct your financial situation, statistics once again show you are only dreaming. Time is of the essence.

You see a few years can erase your debt but it still takes money and time to build true wealth.

The earlier you get serious about your financial profile, the more money you will have to achieve any goal you set for your life.

I'm not trying to bring you down here I truly want you to see that you must start this program as soon as possible and stick with it until you accomplish your goals. Time is ticking away and every day you don't accomplish your goal of becoming debt-free you are losing more money.

My book will show you how to rebuild your future a step at a time, and with only your current income. I'll show you how to reroute your current income and have it work for you, instead of your creditors.

So, now that you've shown you are serious by purchasing this book, and shown you are committed to a debt-free home, let's get to the life changing techniques in this book.

Remember, you will not fail if you simply apply the techniques and remain faithful to them. Your dream of becoming debt-free will become a reality for you.

"Any fact facing us is not as important as our attitude toward it, for that determines our success or failure. The way you think about a fact may defeat you before you ever do anything about it. You are overcome by the fact because you think you are."
Norman Vincent Peale

You're Not Alone

"There are no secrets to success: don't waste time looking for them. Success is the result of perfection, hard work, learning from failure, loyalty to those for whom you work, and persistence."
Colin Powell

I was reluctant to add this part to the book, because it is embarrassing and not something you want everyone to know. It is private information that most are ashamed of and want to keep a secret.

I decided to tell you a shortened version of my debt woe's in order to let you know you're not alone, and there are many people in the same situation as you and there is hope in achieving a debt-free life.

I was a Police Officer for over 12 years and my wife an Office Manager for around 12 years. We made more than double the household median of $49,445 per the Census Bureau. Our combined income averaged around $102,000 per year.

We wanted more out of life and wanted a second home based business. We invested in two rental homes that were financed 100%, 80/20 purchases.

We invested our children's life savings of around $10,000 into life insurance investments.

My mother owned her home but we set her up with an investment taking out around $70,000 of her equity and invested it into two annuities.

I had always paid my bills on time and had an excellent credit score, close to an 800 rating. Then it happened. Anything that could go wrong seemed to go wrong.

The real estate market crashed and our investment properties lost their value. We had evictions for our properties while trying to cover three mortgages. The stock market was plummeting and my mother's investments where losing money.

We couldn't afford to keep paying our children's expensive life insurance policies and so we lost their life savings.

Our business expenses were climbing, and my stress level was at an all-time high. Criminals broke into one of our properties and stole the copper from the home. We had to quickly rehab the property to get it back on the market. The rehab cost thousands of dollars to bring it up to code and back into rent-ready shape.

We never seemed to have any money left over at the end of the month and we felt we were sinking into a black hole.

We restructured our investment property loans which provided a little help. Guess who visited our property again? Yes, you're right, the criminals returned to steal the copper from that home once again.

We were devastated! My once excellent credit was going down the tubes faster than a water slide at the water park.

We decided we could no longer afford to continue to rehab the investment properties especially since they were not supplying us with any form of profit.

Next, we attempted to sell the properties for what was owed on them. Since the real estate market crash, no one was interested.

We then decided to try short-sales on both properties. My new stress levels easily toppled my existing high levels of stress.

I became withdrawn, unhappy and my mind could only think about the bills, how were we going to afford our kid's education? Forget about retiring, and so long to the rich lifestyle we were trying to attain.

We were able to eventually to secure short-sales on both investment properties and were able to settle with the mortgage company, now owing them $10,000 instead of the $130,000 in loans. We fixed my mother's loan, but lost our children's life savings.

Sadly, we still had accumulated over six figures in credit card and unsecured debt, and we didn't know how we were going to pay them off.

We tried for several years to keep up with our debts but in order to save the home we lived in; we were forced to declare bankruptcy.

We had a multitude of personal and business credit cards. Our credit cards had generous limits of over $10,000 and most were maxed out.

Regretfully, we even used my mother's credit card, on which I was a second card holder, just to keep our heads above water.

All of our credit cards were closed due to the Bankruptcy. We had amassed more than $10,000 on my mother's credit card, which still had to be paid since it couldn't be included in the Bankruptcy.

The purchases were necessary for our business and personal expenses. We even paid our personal property tax, totaling over $3,000 with a credit card.

I had to regroup and figure out how to get out of debt quickly, before I died of stress.

I started looking at our bank account and took inventory of where we were spending our money each month.

We began in earnest to cut expenditures on our vehicle insurance bill, cable bill and internet access. We started turning TV's and lights off when they were not in use. In the winter months we turned the heat down and dressed appropriately to stay warm.

In the summer months we used our ceiling fans and turned the air conditioner up to conserve energy. We ate out less, using coupons when we shopped, and we applied the saving each month to our debts.

Within a few months we paid off two credit cards and our only vehicle. I then decided the right thing to do would be to pay off my mother's home, since it was us who got her into another mortgage payment.

We used our tax refunds and other money we received on an injury, to pay down her home, which is now around $16,000 still owed.

We plan to have her home paid off within one year and that will give her a debt-free life.

We are still paying on our home mortgage and helping my mother pay hers as well. We set up our mortgage to be paid biweekly, helping us to pay the mortgage off approximately 8 years earlier, saving us around $80,000.

Once my mother's home is paid in full, we will continue applying our monthly savings to the remaining balance on our mortgage. When our mortgage is paid off we will be debt-free.

So, some readers may say, why should I listen to you? Well, I hope you can see I have made many mistakes trying to better our lives through side businesses, none of which made us any extra money but got us seriously into debt.

We were the "poster child" on how to get into serious debt, and we fell into the 90% statistics bracket of those retiring dead broke. However, we found a way to turn our situation around, and now we have reduced our debt by multiple six figures in a short period of time. We faced stress beyond belief. There we were, in the trenches with those other 89.99% that are deep in debt and having financial trouble.

Trust me; if we can do this, I know you can do it too! It just takes an intense desire to be debt-free, even more than the next unnecessary purchase.

I will share with you the debt reduction plan that we still use to this day so it can help you accomplish your goals. We will not use theory; we will instead, provide you with a roadmap to freedom from debt, that we are still using.

I'm not a financial planner, a tax accountant, insurance agent or counselor, and you should always check with a certified professional before implementing any decision you don't understand or that makes you uncomfortable.

I'm just an average guy who has been through a lesson in debt and didn't like the stress it caused in my life. I have found a way to get out of debt and help anyone who is willing to build true wealth.

I'm not just offering you theory in this book. I'm offering you a tried and true method, one I used every day to get out of debt.

It was important to me to create a book that would help others accomplish a debt-free lifestyle. I could have waited until I was completely debt-free before publishing this book, but the need is too great.

I could have bragged about how I was totally debt-free before writing this book but I thought it more important to get this book into the hands of people that are in pain and need help right now!

I want to be totally honest and not mislead you in any way. We are debt-free except for our mortgage and my mother's mortgage.

Our stress is gone and we have retaken control of our lives. We no longer worry about late credit card payments or where we are going to find money to pay our bills.

It is truly liberating, and has improved our marriage, our family relationships, and we are finally sleeping through the night again.

One of the most important factors in your success is to make a total commitment to follow the techniques in the book until you reach your ultimate goal of debt-free living.

Without a serious commitment to your own well-being and without taking action on the techniques I'm sharing with you, this book it will be nothing more than another book you've added to your collection.

Another important factor to consider is to talking to your spouse or significant other and getting them on board with your plan. Discuss with them your plan for the future of our family and stress how important it is that you work together to achieve this goal.

In doing this you will be united with each other and able to support each other until you're successful. If one of you is having a bad day or starting to slip, you have the support of the other in place so you can get back on track as quickly as possible.

So next, let's take a look at why most of us got into debt in the first place.

How Did I Get Into This Mess?

"The state of your life is nothing more than a reflection of your state of mind."
Dr. Wayne W. Dyer

Karen was a smart girl, graduating high school with a 3.8 grade point average. Karen followed the advice of her parents and started college at a private university. She needed a car to get back and forth to college, so her parents co-signed on her new loan for a new vehicle. Karen finished college and graduated school with over $80,000 in student loans.

She met her life-long mate, Jack at school and they married upon their graduation. Jack and Karen found jobs near Karen's parents but they needed a new home for their new lives.

They didn't have any money saved and borrowed a down payment from Karen's parents. Jack and Karen didn't have the necessary down payment to avoid PMI (Private Mortgage Insurance) so that amount was added to their monthly payments.

Life was looking up, or so they thought. Now that they were in their new home, it was necessary to finance the furniture necessary to complete their new dream home. After all, they were starting their new lives together as a family.

The couple financed $13,000 to buy new furniture. They heard a commercial advertising "no payments for 24 months" and got excited about their good fortune. Now they could furnish their home in style.

Then Jack needed a new car to get back and forth to work every day, and he leased a new vehicle because the payments advertised were cheaper, only $400 per month for a new Chrysler 300!

Jack and Karen's combined income came to the same amount as the national average, approximately $50,000 dollars annually per the census bureau.

Now they were deluged with credit card applications. They both wanted to build their credit and were accepted with 5 different credit card companies.

Within a year Karen became pregnant and they were so excited to be starting a family.

Jack and Karen decided to take a vacation, after all, once the baby arrives, there may not be any traveling for a few years.

Jack used his new credit card to fund a 1 week Caribbean Cruise that cost them $3,000.

Once they returned from their awesome vacation it was time to upgrade the baby's room with a new paint job and carpet. They also needed a crib, car seats, bassinets, strollers and all the other little items totaling another $5,000, all placed on a credit card.

Jack and Karen were now living the American dream and were one happy family until Karen lost her job in the cutbacks. They agreed it wouldn't be worth looking for a new job, at least not until they had their baby.

Jack and Karen's salary quickly dropped to $30,000 a year. They were in debt up to their eyeballs and didn't know how they were going to pay the bills.

The above story is one that is very common for the 90% of the families and individuals that are in debt. A common question most people ask is, "How did I get into all this debt?"

Let's start by saying; it's not completely your fault. High schools and colleges don't teach students how to live without debt, and most parents are just as ill-informed as their children. I feel that this is one of the major reasons 90% of the population is in debt and must retire broke.

Since we are not taught how to live a debt-free way of life, we look to others and gravitate to what others are doing. We all want to be "normal," have what the next guys has and continue "Keeping up with the Joneses."

With the constant bombardment of advertising telling us what to do and what to buy it's hard not to buckle under the pressure.

Commercials tell us we deserve it, you can have it with only low, affordable monthly payments. Bring your tax check in and you can drive away with a car -- today. Bad credit? No problem!

Karen and Jack are just doing what everyone else is doing. They want a similar life to what everyone else seems to have, and it is one of debt.

They finished college, but they weren't taught to delay gratification. Jack and Karen wouldn't be in a debt situation if someone had helped them understand they could be rich if they had gotten an apartment, saved their paychecks and applied all they could afford toward their student loans first.

Once the loans were paid off, save enough down payment to avoid expensive PMI insurance, which could have made the cost of their home a lot cheaper.

Some mortgage companies won't remove the PMI insurance even after you meet the required 20% down payment required. Most people forget to request that the insurance be removed once they meet the required condition.

Jack and Karen should never have leased a vehicle; there are far too many specifications required. Leases are loaded with fees you must follow specifically.

It would have been better for Jack to have purchased a 2-3 year old vehicle and it could have been his, with no payments in a relatively short time.

Even better, jack could have saved enough money to pay cash for the vehicle and avoid any extra interest charges to finance the purchase.

When Karen lost her job, it would have been much easier for them to make it on just Jack's income, if their student loans and Jack's vehicle were already paid in full. Karen might have found it necessary to go back to work and enjoyed raising their baby at home. How many individuals get to do that without severe sacrifice today?

Jack and Karen could be living a debt-free life style if they had known how. So you see it's not always entirely our fault when we have financial problems.

Next, we will look at some other reasons that are not obvious but do play a part in our getting into debt. There are forces behind the scenes that once are brought to our attention, can help us save us money. The following are enemies of a debt-free lifestyle.

It's Not Your Fault

"From now on, change will be the constant. The individuals best prepared to succeed are those who can learn, modify, and grow, regardless of age, experience, or ego."
Danny Goodman

We are inundated every day with commercials urging us to buy, and to buy the newest, latest, and greatest gadgets etc. Being human, we want what everyone else has. We have an innate desire to fit in and sometimes we reason that everyone else is buying a house with a 30-year mortgage; and I desire the same things that everyone else has.

Credit card companies send you new credit card applications every day in the mail. Think about it, every advertiser is hoping their ads will do a good job in getting you to purchase their product and they'll get some of your money.

It is hard to make excellent purchasing decisions and stay debt-free because there is no real training in personal money management. High schools and colleges teach specific criteria to help prepare you for a degree in a specific type of career. Where is the training on how to keep more of your money, make smarter consumer purchases and build true wealth? There are socio-economic factors at work all around us that are not very obvious to our conscious minds. Most of these factors are ingrained in our subconscious.

So, up to this point it hasn't been your fault. Once you read this book and understand why you are possibly in debt, then your choices will rest on your shoulders. I want to dare you to be different than the 90% of individuals retiring dead broke and still in debt. Dare to be one of the 10% that owns their own life and can retire with no worries about money or how to pay for the lifestyle you desire when you retire.

Let's now take a look at the factors we seldom think of that are causing us to over spend and get into so much debt.

Herd Mentality

"You can't win without being completely different. When everyone else says we are crazy, I say, gee we must be on to something."
Larry D. Ellison

What is the herd mentality and what do I mean by it? Herd mentality is when we as a society, want to be around other people just like us. We want to be accepted by others and to be like them.

What thought comes to mind when you think of purchasing a new home? It might be "Well, everyone else is buying a house and financing it." Not considering that almost everyone else is in debt.

It's not that you shouldn't purchase your new dream home, it's how and when you purchase it that matters.

Saving an adequate down payment, would be ideal in order to avoid the expensive PMI insurance. After you purchase your new home, using accelerated payments to pay your mortgage can save you thousands of dollars in interest payments over the life of the loan.

This, in turn could be applied to investments which can help to build true wealth.

We also see others buying new cars and appearing to be wealthy. Most of those people are broke too, because of keeping up the appearance of wealth.

Most Millionaires' are frugal, buying 2-3 year old vehicles with cash and driving them until the wheel's fall off. They delay gratification and don't make purchases until they can afford to pay cash for them.

There is another excellent book called "The Millionaire Next Door" by Thomas J. Stanley, Ph.D. and William D. Danko, Ph.D. that provide some excellent ideas on how these normal appearing individuals become super rich.

The herd mentality is one that most people follow without thinking, about the debt it causes. In our self-talk we tell ourselves in our minds, telling ourselves that everyone else is doing it and we deserve to do it too.

Jack and Karen are great examples of the herd mentality. Jack and Karen did not see how quickly they were getting into deep debt.

Jack needed another car, he's seeing so many others driving nice cars.

Jack is aware he now has a good job and he has to get to work every day and wants to impress people with a nice car when he pulls up for an appointment.

Notice that I stated he wants to impress people. Jack really cannot afford the payments however; he wants people to see him as successful.

This brings me to the next reason we get into debt.

Keeping Up With the Joneses

Keeping up with the Joneses causes another form of crippling debt. We may often visit a friend's house and see new furniture, a nice patio set with a wood-burning fire place, and a new Corvette in their driveway.

We instantly get a feeling of wow! They have nicer stuff than me. Subconsciously we think we need to update our patio furniture and we need a nice new car. Why does our mind tell us these things?

Our minds are constantly working, telling us that we have to get similar things to be accepted and to stay accepted by our friends.

Most of us also tend to feel like we deserve the same things that our friends have. An attitude that "I work hard, I deserve to treat myself to the finer things in life" is common for individuals in debt.

The problem lies in that the Joneses more than likely are living a life financed to the hilts. What you don't see is that appearing rich is all that the Joneses have.

Their lives are full of stress, never knowing if they are about to lose their new car; their home, how they are never going to have enough money to retire. Unfortunately, many are looking or have looked into filing for bankruptcy.

The Joneses outward appearance is one of riches, living a happy life with fancy toys. They may appear to have their lives together; and this gives everyone around them a false sense of reality.

So, since the majority of people emulate their friends and want to be accepted; they tend to repeat the behavior of their seemingly successful friends.

Unfortunately they have only achieved a debt-filled life and have become one of the 90% in heavy debt, per the statistics of the Census bureau.

Now we can begin to see where these are unconscious decisions we make and that it really isn't anyone's fault even though it affects the quality of our lives.

We don't start out thinking, "Oh, let's get ourselves into enough debt to cripple ourselves and retire broke." No, we just see everyone we associate with, getting cool new things and we want them too.

We also feel that we deserve them, instead of delay gratification; we go ahead and purchase them anyway, with credit.

In the next section we will look at advertising and how it affects our purchasing decisions.

The Advertising Trap

We're all so familiar with advertisements that we see and hear every day; we hear them on the radio and when we turn on the television.

Some commercials are so overbearing that as soon as you hear one of them, you immediately recognize the song or jingle, and often we can finish their sentences.

The advertisers hit us with a myriad of choices such as new cars, cologne, insurance, vacations, cruises, infomercials that advertise the newest gadgets to make your life easier, weight loss programs, education programs and the list goes on and on.

Marketers are excellent at making their commercials funny, exciting, and sexy. They know exactly how to sell their products and services and they know how to get your hard earned money.

Top businesses spend millions on just one 30-second commercial to air during the Super Bowl. What does that mean? It means they are making a lot more money from the ad than what they spent in advertising in a 30-second commercial.

Again, it really is not your fault! We see our favorite actors, actresses, and reality shows stars driving fancy cars, living in expensive mansions and spending money on cruises and exotic vacations. These movies, commercials and radio advertisements give the appearance of a happy, exciting, successful lifestyle when it's really just advertising.

Advertisers know how to sell you on their products by offering a low monthly payment or slyly telling you how you deserve it and if you put it on your credit card, you can have it today!

We fall right into their trap and begin telling ourselves that we do deserve a better. We tell ourselves, "After all, I work hard and want to live a life that is fun and exciting too."

We've seen that in order to be like others and live an exciting life that appears to be fun and exciting will only lead us into more unsecured credit debt than we can afford. When we succumb to these purchases, our credit limit declines and we begin to max out our credit cards.

All advertising experts make us desire what they are selling. These companies hire the top marketing people to design commercials that will bring in a lot of sales. If their efforts don't work they return to the drawing board and come up with a better idea, one that will sell!

Some marketing companies do something called spilt-testing. They make a couple of commercials with slight differences and then track where the purchases come from.

They use different telephone numbers on each one and when customers call they are able to track which commercial is performing the best. This tells them the conversion rate of each and how to structure their future ads.

Most people never consider what is actually happening behind the scenes. We just do what most others do and fall into the advertising trap and continue making many unnecessary purchases.

We then turn to our credit card statement and have sticker shock! "How did I spend this much money and wind up with this much debt?" Mindless buying is where we can get into huge trouble.

I do know that individuals will have needs and that some purchases are necessary. Those purchases are not being considered here. The purchases we are discussing in this section are needless, impulse buying, for what we want not what we need.

I'm not saying you can't purchase most of these items; you'll need a strategic plan for those purchases. Just make sure you are making those purchases on your terms and not the seller's terms.

I want you to be aware there are unseen forces working against a debt-free lifestyle but once you're aware of the pitfalls it makes saying no to rampant advertising much easier.

Credit Is Killing Your Debt-Free Lifestyle

"Capital as such is not evil; it is wrong use that is evil."
Mohandas Gandhi

Unsecure credit can be great for someone with discipline and a financial plan. For others unsecured credit is death on their financial future.

The statistics state that the average credit card debt per household in American is over $15,000. The Survey of Consumer Payment Choice, Federal Reserve Bank of Boston, in January 2010 states there are 609.9 credit cards help by U.S. consumers alone and at the end of 2008 the average consumer held 3.5 credit cards.

The average APR (annual percentage rate) is 12.78% but can quickly increase with one late payment. Federal Reserve's G-19 report on consumer credit, released in February 2012 states the total U.S. consumer debt is $2.5 Trillion with a T as of December 2011.

Longtime credit card industry advisor R.K. Hammer, stated in a report dated June 2011 that credit card company's fees peaked in 2009 at a staggering $22.9 Billion dollars. That number indicates fees only related to the credit card, not the interest charged on those accounts.

In a report from December 2009, FINRA Investor Education Foundation, "Financial Capability in the United States," stated 41% of cardholders between the ages of 18 to 29 made only the minimum payment required on a credit card during the past 12 months.

BSC Alliance (dot) com states "The credit card industry is the most profitable one in the United States with annual earnings in the $30 Billion dollar range. Many people might be surprised to learn that a single credit card issuer – MBNA – earned 1.5 times more profit than McDonalds in 2004.

Citibank, another major credit card issuer, earns more profit than both Microsoft and Wal-Mart."

With statistics like these how can anyone truly believe they are going to have a debt-free lifestyle? Credit card companies are getting rich on our backs.

If we, as a society don't learn the true cost of items we purchase and if we don't implement a debt reduction program, we are going to get to retirement age and still have to work through our golden years.

Statistics show that most consumers in the U.S. have at least 3 credit cards, which allow them to make impulse purchases. Credit card companies want to give you credit. They know that the more money they lend the more profit they will receive.

Who really thinks about their credit cards as being a Billion dollar business? We just think that it is a way to get what we want when we want it. We don't really weigh what it really costs to make an impulse purchases on items we really don't need. These are the types of purchases that are keeping you from eliminating your debt and building your wealth instead of filing the pockets of the credit card companies.

If you feel credit cards are hard to resist like so many others have, then you should close your accounts and cut your credit cards up and throw them away.

You may opt to keep one credit card open for dire emergencies only. Keeping one credit card open can provide you with a feeling of security while you are working toward your debt reduction.

I suggest taking it out of your wallet or purse and keep it in a safe secure environment, somewhere that is hard to get to, to avoid impulse purchasing.

The point here is to keep it open for a real emergency situation but don't keep it with you when you're out and about shopping. You will be tempted all the time to just put this one purchase on the card and then rationalize that you will quickly pay it off.

The next thing you know you're right back into more debt. Remember these purchases don't seem all that bad by themselves but when you get the bill have you ever stated to yourself, "WOW, how did I spend all that money, it only seemed like a few things?" When you continue to carry your credit card it makes impulse purchases too easy and you'll probably continue to do what you've always done through the years that got you into debt.

Credit card companies outwardly appear to be helping you when you enroll with a credit card that offers cash back or frequent flyer miles, right?

Wrong! They offer these programs to get deeper into debt with their card. In order to earn those miles or get cash back you have to use their card. They hope you won't be able to pay the full amount off each month, which starts to create wealth for them not you.

When you receive a credit card with a credit limit of say, $6,000 it is a borrowing limit that comes with a high interest price tag. You see, they are not giving you $6,000.

They are giving you a convenient way to make them rich by using their cash advances. If you don't have the money, but you make the purchases on their card, you will not only pay for that item plus interest, but you will also be paying with money you have not yet earned. You will be paying debt with money you have yet to see.

When you are financing your lifestyle with credit everything you purchase cost you more. You pay for the product or service once and continue to pay interest on that purchase until the card returns to a $0.00 balance.

For most people it never returns to zero and for those people they will pay for each purchase at least three times, maybe four, before it is paid off.

Credit card companies are working against your financial freedom every day. They seem to be helping you by offering low minimum payments. "Oh," we think, "How nice, they care about us and want to make our purchases affordable."

Behind the scenes they are happy to offer low monthly minimums on payments, because they profit more when you only make minimum payments. Oh, and don't forget if you are ever late and were one of the lucky ones to have a low APR credit card offer, be aware that it will quickly disappear and jump to 20% or more interest.

Cha Ching! They just increased their profits and you still think your low monthly payment is very convenient for you. All the while they are taking more of your minimum payment as profit and keeping you in debt for a longer period of time. And you decide you only want to pay the minimum payment every month until the debt is gone.

Taking an average credit card percentage rate of 12.78%, and the average household credit card debt of $15,000, with no additional purchases, and you only pay a 2% minimum toward your monthly payment, this payment totals around $300.00 per month.

If you make all the payments on time, it is estimated that it will take you 30 years to repay the credit card. You will have paid a total of $31,382 over those 30 years.

The summary breaks down to paying the original $15,000 and over 2 times the original purchase price, giving the credit card company a huge profit of $16,382. The calculations in this example were calculated by the Federal Reserve credit card calculator.

Just think, if you didn't need those items you purchased with credit and could have waited and paid cash for them, you could have invested that extra $16,382 and made it grow into substantial wealth. This example represents the average person per the statistics, and I think it reveals why individuals retire dead broke.

It is the 10% that retire wealthy that understand that you can't finance your life into the future. The buy now, pay later attitude can cost you severely.

The credit card companies don't even send you a thank you letter for making them rich while you gave away all your hard-earned money to them.

The items you originally purchase are probably broken, outdated, or no longer of value to you. Those items were very expensive to your overall net worth.

Now that I have brought this to your attention, can you see how the credit card companies don't really care about your needs, but are really there to make them money and not to help you?

They want every person that can't delay gratification as their customer, for they tend to purchase things they cannot afford.   Its big money in their pockets so they love to get the credit cards in as many people's hands as possible.

Some individuals fall right into the credit card company's plan, when they see they are close to reaching enough miles to get a free airline ticket, so they make unnecessary purchases to meet the cards requirements.

Most of these cards limit what airline, hotel chain and so forth that you can spend your credits or tickets on.

Imagine going shopping with your family and enjoying the day together. You can have an excellent time together without the need to blow money on useless items you think you need, but quickly lose their excitement.

The goal is to stop spending on credit and start working on paying those high interest credit cards as quickly as possible. The only way to become completely debt-free is to get 100% out of debt and stop living on borrowed money.

If you continue to make purchases using credit instead of cash, you will only perpetuate debt into your life further and you won't have a chance at real freedom from debt.

Right now you may not believe you can live without credit. You've become accustomed to purchasing with credit cards for years. At first this may seem hard at first, but once you pay off your first credit card, then your second you'll start to wonder why you ever used them to begin with.

Giving up credit cards is one of the most important and rewarding steps you can take toward becoming debt-free.

An excellent way to still purchase items you need is to get yourself a debit card from your bank. Debit cards look just like a credit card but limit you to only purchasing items you can afford to purchase.

It is like using cash since the money comes directly out of your checking account, but keeps you to from carrying a lot of cash around in your pocket.

Using a debit card can help you learn how to budget your money and live within a cash only lifestyle that we all need to focus on.

If you follow this plan it won't take you long to build up more cash in your life.

Can you image in just a few short years you can be out of debt and keep most of your paycheck.   You can save for an emergency fund, begin to save to build wealth, or have the freedom to do with it what you want. So, if I can get you to take action and start wiping out your unsecured debt, you will be well on your way to a happy, fulfilling lifestyle.

It may appear now, to be a hard task to accomplish, but applying more of your resources to your debts and paying your bills with cash will become easier with time.

Later in the book we will look at the plan you'll be following that will quickly begin freeing up more money every month than you ever thought possible.

Each debt you pay off will free up a monthly payment that is keeping you in debt. The quicker you pay off your credit cards the quicker you can become debt-free and start to build wealth.

Having spending habits of unnecessary purchases and financing them with credit is costing you your future wealth.

Most tend to rationalize what they buy until one day it's too late, then they are ready to retire and owe too much money to retire. They scratch their heads and wonder what happened to them. I thought I would have paid these debts off long ago, but there just never was enough money and now that I'm ready to retire I can't. This is not the lifestyle we desire but statistics prove it is realistic for 90% of the population.

I know you don't want the above situation to become a reality for your and your family and I know you desire to be in the 10% statistic that retires financially secure.

If you take action now, you will be able to enjoy retirement and have enough money to enjoy the life in your golden years.

There is an old saying, "People don't plan to fail, they simply fail to plan is true for the 90% of people retiring broke or working until they pass away. If you set this simple plan in motion, stay dedicated to it, there is no doubt in my mind you can achieve a debt free lifestyle and then build true wealth.

Just think of all the money you could save if you owned your home, had no vehicle payments, no credit cards or unsecure debt due each month.

You could quickly build a nice nest egg. The quicker you decide to become debt-free and achieve that goal the more wealth you will be able to create in your lifetime.

You have been paying your life forward with the future money you have yet to earn. If you can stop that spending spiral and pay off those high interest credit cards, you will have more money to invest in your future.

Another benefit you may not have thought of is the fact that you can purchase more of the things you want and need than those people who solely rely on credit.

If two people make the same purchases, but one uses credit and the other pays with cash, the person paying with cash can afford to purchase more things or invest his savings. Here is an example:

Bob and Joe both purchase the same style big screen television and pay the same price of $3,000. Bob pays the $3,000 with his credit card. Joe uses his debit card and pays for the television with the cash in his account.

Over the lifetime of the loan, Bob will be paying $3,000 + around $834 dollars in interest payments making the TV really cost him $3834.

Joe owned the same television immediately upon purchase and only paid the actual value of $3,000.

Bob and Joe later decided to purchase the same pickup truck for $30,000. If Bob pays the same way he has been paying and finances his life forward, he could pay an extra $7,000-$10,000 dollars, depending on the interest rate, for the same truck Joe purchased with cash.

Now as you can see that if Bob always finances his life forward, he has less spending dollars that Joe and Joe can actually afford to purchase more or invest the difference that Bob is spending on every purchase he finances with credit.

Just in the two examples above Joe now has $7,834 more than Bob, even though they both have the same items.

As mentioned, the credit card companies are not handing you $5,000. That is your spending limit. All purchases must be repaid and if you make purchases without being able to pay that amount off, not only are you risking legal action on their part to recoup their money, you are also making purchases with future money yet to be earned.

Of course you know that you will be repaying a lot more than the original purchase for the same items that others decided to pay cash for.

When I figured out how much credit was truly costing me I decided I couldn't afford to use it anymore. I canceled my credit cards and paid them all off. I then cut them up and celebrated! I knew I had figured out the missing link to being broke and living in debt.

In the next session we'll talk about another thing that isn't your fault but causes so many individuals to get into debt.

Who Teaches Us to Live a Debt-Free Lifestyle?

"There are three ingredients in the good life: Learning, earning and yearning."
Christopher Morley

While I was worrying about all my own debt, I thought back to my college years and can't think of one class that offered training on how to live a debt-free lifestyle.

Then I started thinking, who teaches us to live a debt-free lifestyle? No one and that's part of the problem. I can't believe that we spend thousands, if not hundreds of thousands of dollars on a college degree and never receive one of the most important lessons in life, and that's training on how to stay out of debt and live within our means.

If someone understood debt-free living and only earned a small salary during their lifetime they could still retire rich, with millions of dollars in the bank.

If an individual was able to invest $45,000 by age 25 in a tax sheltered Index fund with an annual rate of return of only 8%, they could retire at age 65 with an estimated $1,092,302.34 (This figure was computed with MS Financial Savvy's online calculator).

Can you image the results if you were to keep that menial paying job over those 40 years and you only added a mere $100 a month to your initial investment?

You would wind up with an estimated $1,611,447.63. You would profit by another $519,145.30. You may want to go to MS

Financial Savvy's website or the Bank Rate website and play with their calculators.

If you continued to invest even a small amount of money every month with a menial paying job you could retire with more money than many doctors and lawyers. They would love to have that amount of money in the bank instead of where most wind up.

I started thinking, why is it then that the top salary earners are also retiring dead broke? They make huge salaries and still aren't retiring rich.

Now I must say that some of the top salary earners may be in the top 10%, but with that 90% ratio of people retiring at age 65 deep in debt and unable to claim a financially independent lifestyle, there are quite a few of the high income earners that are also in debt.

Most of these high salary earners have at least a Bachelor's degree and some have a Master's or Ph.D. As you can see, there is no one is teaching even the most affluent of us on how to stay out of debt or how to build true wealth.

It is shocking to believe that everyone has the same chance of becoming a millionaire and retiring financially independent. It's just that statistics prove that most don't ever gain the knowledge or understand the concepts in this book.

Once again, they have spent a long time in school and believe they are entitled to the comfort of an above average income.

They believe they should be able to spend their money when ever and where ever they please. However, if someone had given them these principles at an early age, I think most would have changed their thinking about paying cash for their lifestyles instead of gratification now and getting into debt.

It goes to show how marketing, credit cards, keeping up with the Joneses, lack of training in financial education, and the herd mentality can get us into debt. You can probably see now that it isn't your fault. The above forces are working against you every day, but they are also promoted to us as good and helpful things for us.

I've revealed these truths to you and you are aware of what is really going on, now it is up to you to change your mentality and financial future.

At this point you have two choices. You can chose to become financially responsible and wind up one of the 10% that are financially independent or you can choose to do nothing and wind up one of the 90% that are in debt, stressed out and unable to retire in your golden years.

It is my goal to help everyone I can but it still comes down to your choice. Next, we will be covering how to strategically apply some simple strategies that if followed with determination can have you out of debt within a handful of years.

This is my goal for you. If you are serious about changing your financial future, you must vow to not give up until you are debt-free.

We will only be using your current income in this scenario. If you want to increase your income and apply the difference to your debts, you will be able to shorten the date by which you will be debt free.

We can even complete your debt free program without a true budget. We are simply going to follow a few simple principles, have accountability and more importantly, show determination.

You have to work at this program and apply the principles to your life or you will not be successful. If you do apply these principles and techniques and if your debt is average, you will become debt-free within a handful of years from the time you begin to take action.

Situations vary as does the estimated time of when you are free from debt. Either way, your determination and implementation of the techniques will produce results.

It is also important to not delay your start date. You may talk yourself into starting soon but you decide to delay your stating date until after you make a few more important purchases.

The reasoning will only delay your long awaited freedom from debt making you waste future investment dollars every day you wait. Urgency is of extreme importance! The faster you start and stay the course, the faster you will achieve your goals.

So, now that we know how we got into debt, let's take a look at how to turn the tables on debt and reverse the compounding interest charged by credit card companies that is hurting you. Turning it around, compound interest can help you get out of debt much faster.

Why Pay Off My Mortgage

Most individuals will say, "Why should I pay off my mortgage, I've got a great interest rate of only 5%?"

Did you know that if you paid your home in full within the first year you would experience a true rate of 5% interest?

I'm guessing you never did the math on what you really pay over the course of your loan. Let's take an average mortgage loan amount of $170,000.

$170,000 x 5% = $8,500

If you pay your monthly mortgage amount of $900 dollars every month over the course of your 30-year fixed mortgage, you will have paid $158,534 in interest alone over the course of the loan.

The total cost of your home in this scenario would have cost you $328,534. At this rate, you will have paid nearly double the original cost of $170,000.

You should also realize if you didn't have 20% down payment you probably are paying additional money for mortgage insurance. This payment doesn't help you in any way. It simply is an insurance policy that protects the bank if you default on your loan.

PMI insurance is very expensive and when you reach the 20% equity in your home you could stop paying this extra monthly expense that is sometimes added into your payment.

If you don't request they remove the PMI insurance when you reach the 80% amount on your mortgage, you may find you're still paying for this insurance, and will continue to pay until you request they stop billing you.

By looking at your monthly mortgage coupon you can determine the true percent of your payment that actually decreases your principle balance.

On an amortized monthly payment of $2,076, $818 goes to pay the interest while only $258 is applied to the principle.

That is a true 76% interest rate not 5% – 6%. Some individuals may be paying as much as 90% interest rate on their loan.

Mortgage companies typically use the accounting method called the rule of 78's, meaning your payment is geared toward the principle declining as the loan is paid off.

Again, we are following the herd and doing what everyone else is doing. We just assume we have an excellent interest rate and will pay our house off like everyone else does in thirty years.

If we see that the majority of the herd is in the 90% statistic that retires in debt and possibly broke, we know we have to do something different.

Neither the stock market, nor any other investment I know of will provide you with a rate of return like paying down that 76% interest rate.

Every dollar you apply to your loan is providing you with a real 76% rate of return. You are actually realizing a savings of 76% in interest.

If someone follows the techniques in this book and they pay off their mortgage in a handful of years and someone else decides to keep their mortgage, and then they both lose their jobs, which person will have an easier time financially without an income?

You see, when you are debt-free your expenses greatly decrease and you can survive on less money per month.

If you pay off your mortgage before starting an investment plan, you can save a large portion of that $158,534 in the above example.

For someone who chooses not to pay off their home first and continues to invest trying to make money, they are going to pay that $158,534. Do you think your investments will yield the $158,534 you're paying out in interest? If your answer is no, you have already lost money and you aren't living the stress-free, debt-free life you envisioned for yourself.

If you focus on paying your home off within a handful of years you will have realized a savings of approximately $158,534 but you don't have any real money invested.

I will be explaining in more detail how the techniques work. For now, let's just say that you will have more and more money each month as each debt is paid off. When the mortgage is paid in full you will have all your income to invest or do with it as you will.

I've found that most people have around $2,000 to invest each month. Let's assume they paid all their debts off, including their home.

Taking that $2,000 a month that was being used to pay the mortgage and other bills; they then decide to invest it in an account with a return of around 5%.

That investment over the course of the same twenty three years as opposed to another person, who kept paying on their mortgage, could earn for the first investor and estimated $1,055,201.18 in that 23 year period.

I hope you are seeing how important it is to pay all debts, including your mortgage, as quickly as possible. It is the fastest way to accumulate real wealth.

Think about how much easier it would be to own your home and have no debts. Where will you be if you don't follow the plan and eliminate your debts?

Aren't you tired of the stress and aren't you also tired of fighting over the bills with your spouse or significant other? So how are you going to pay for them?

Statistics also show that stress over money and paying bills is one of the biggest reasons couples argue.

When all your debts are paid in full you have created choices for where and when you work.

Even if you keep your mortgage you'll have to continue doing what is necessary to make those payments until it is paid in full.

It is important to show your significant other the statistics and run the numbers for yourselves. It should be a goal to get on the same page with your significant other and provide support for each other in order to crush your debt and build wealth.

It will be harder to achieve the wealth you deserve if someone is constantly pulling against your efforts on achieving your goals.

Like-minded people set their goals together so they can approach debt together, structure their plan of attack and support each other along the journey.

Don't worry if your significant other isn't on the same page or is even reluctant. You can still follow the system, you will just have to stay firm in your plan and work the system yourself. You can do it, have faith and you will persevere.

Can you now see the importance of eliminating your debts as quickly as possible? It is the best way to build wealth for the long term and retire financially free.

Once you eliminate debt, you will have the necessary money to invest and build wealth. Trying to eliminate debt and invest at the same time reduces the amount of your investing dollars, keeps you in debt, paying more than you have too and sacrificing future investment dollars that can build true wealth.

It appears that only 10% of the financially independent individuals understand these simple to implement techniques.

They are not a part of the herd mentality, instead they have chosen to do something different and own their lives.

They usually are the ones that live below their means or within their needs and delay gratification in order to build their wealth.

They understand that debt cannot make them wealthy and will only hurt any chance they have at financial freedom.

They are doers, people that take action.

They are individuals that know they alone are responsible for their retirement and they'll do whatever is necessary to secure their financial success.

You may think of these individuals as the Hollywood elite, but you'd be wrong.

These people own their vehicles outright, because they pay cash when they purchase them. They purchase two to three year old vehicles to avoid the heavy depreciation of a new vehicle.

They shop for bargains, never paying for over priced items.

They pay their homes off early. They don't buy watches, fancy clothes; sports cars and homes they can't afford to impress others with an outward appearance of seeming rich.

They are your neighbors; they are normal, average looking people who are making smart decisions with their money.

Most people will make over a million dollars in their lifetime. It's what you decide to do with the money that counts.

If you allow credit card companies, mortgage companies, car dealership, and big ticket sellers to have all your money or if you pay more for everything you purchase because you want it now, you are probably destined to never keep any of it.

The majority of those you see that appear to be millionaires, driving the expensive sports cars, living in the huge mansions, and taking expensive vacations, seldom own their lives and probably have a huge debt load to carry.

They can't afford those things, but are willing to live in debt in order to live a rich lifestyle. They made a decision to rent their lifestyle with a line of credit in order to look like they're rich.

If all those individuals seem rich, are the statistics lying when they show that at least 90% of them will at retirement age, retire in debt, broke or both?

Are you seeing that, we have preconceived ideas of what millionaires look like because of seeing them through reality television, and commercials?

We assume they are rich and can afford anything they want. I've never heard any of those people on those shows say they were debt-free. We assume by the way they lead their lives and the things they do on those shows that they have millions in the bank and are financially free.

I'm not saying that some of them aren't millionaires, but will it ever be you making that kind of money or have a television show that pays millions a years? If so, that is awesome, just remember to stay out of debt and you will be far ahead of the rest of us.

Most of us have normal jobs and will have to make our dreams come true with the money we have available to us.

Make the decision today to break free from the herd mentality, do something different, change your behaviors and secure your financial freedom.

Once you become debt free, you own your life and all the things you've purchased. Doesn't that sound like the dream we all desire. Owning our lives, living stress free and having cash to invest for our future is the sum of all of our dreams.

You can have those things in only a few short years, if you decide today to start this program, knuckle down and make it happen for you and your family.

I have faith in you and know that it has been the advertising, lack of education, credit card companies, mortgages and the herd mentality that has gotten you into debt.

It's time for you to step up and become accountable for where you are, declare that you are going to change your financial plan for your life, set a new goal, have determination and take action.

Boom! A handful of years later and you're debt free with cash flowing into your life, and you're investing for your future. You have achieved what 90% of most people never will. Financial Freedom and Prosperity!

Tips for Success

"I find it fascinating that most people plan their vacation with better care than they do their lives. Perhaps that is because escape is easier than change."
Jim Rohn

It is very important to change your current mindset. You are going to have to avoid impulse purchases. Don't fall for the low easy payment options, avoid going to places where you may make impulse purchases like the shopping mall. You may want to cut down on eating out as much as you currently are or making a decision to treat yourself and your family only once a month. Just remember that every dollar you can save and put towards your debt will help you achieve your goals quicker.

One of the most important factors for you in accomplishing your goal's, is to have determination and follow through on your commitment.

Don't give up once you start. Once you pay your first credit card off, I think you'll start to get excited. Let that excitement build and keep you focused and determined. I know when I paid my first credit card off and I started to want it more and even quicker. I started thinking of anything and everything I could to save more money.

I looked at saving on our car and home insurance, stopped eating out so much, cut our grocery bill in half and starting using coupons. I turned off the television when it wasn't being watched but was just used for noise in the room. It's much cheaper to use the radio if you just want to hear noise.

I could barely wait to get my tax return money and apply it to a debt. I had an injury check coming that I applied to a debt. When I knew I could get out of debt, I had an "I want out of debt now" attitude.

I thought of it as being at war with debt and I wasn't going to lose. I want to be in the 10% of financially independent people by the time I retire.

I put into place a support group consisting of my wife and two daughters. Having support in your family can teach your children the techniques in this book and help them learn while they're young. They can have a better chance at building wealth at an earlier age than you did.

If your spouse or significant other is on the same page, your debt reduction program will be a lot easier than fighting against someone you love to accomplish your goals.

Although this may sound silly, I made a saying that "I will delay gratification today, so I can have wealth tomorrow." Copy mine or make your own and say it every day.

Having a saying like this keeps your goals in your minds and reassures you that you are on track and correcting with your life. It also reminds you every day there is an end in sight and with a great outcome. I'll be able to do anything I want and live a life others only dream about.

If you start to feel down or lose a little ground, don't give up, shake off the dust and get right back in the game. The only reason you won't achieve this type of debt free lifestyle will be YOU! Everything you need to succeed is right here.

Another important tip is to close all your credit cards except one that you'll keep for emergencies. When you close those accounts cut up the credit cards and rejoice because they are no longer getting you into more debt.

Not using credit anymore is very important to your future. We are going to be using the compound principle they use to keep you in debt to snowball you out of debt at an accelerated rate.

"This one step – choosing a goal and sticking to it – changes everything."

Scott Reed

Crush It! Crush Your Debt Plan

"You have to put in many, many, many tiny efforts that nobody sees or appreciates before you achieve anything worthwhile."
Brian Tracy

We need to first start by finding some extra money will be applied to the first debt. I suggest using at least 10% of your gross income to apply to what we will call your monthly Debt Elimination Fund (DEF). We will take the average household combined income of $50,000 per year. If we divide that into 26 payments throughout the year, the average family makes approximately $1923 per pay check. Now if we take 10% of $1923, we will have approximately $192 dollars as our starting DEF.

You can also apply any other money that you save by implementing any of the above saving techniques. If you eat out 4 times a week and spend $30 per meal it would total $120 a week or $480 per month.

You might decide to only eat out once a month so you can apply more money to your debts. You would take the $480 spent per month minus $30 you intend to spend and that equals $450 savings per month.

Now take the $450 per month in savings and add it to the 10% DEF, which totaled $192 and you have $642 DEF to apply to the first credit card.

Once your first unsecured debt (credit card) is paid off, we will take the minimum payment you were paying on that card and add that to our DEF. Each debt that is paid off will increase the DEF now that compounding is used in your favor, instead of being used against you.

As more and more debts are paid off your DEF will quickly grow. As this DEF grows and you apply it to the bills that are left, you will be paying your debts down at a significant rate.

You will continue to pay each unsecure debt until they are gone. You will then start paying the DEF to your mortgage and you are on your way to a debt-free lifestyle.

Organizing Your Debts

Take out a sheet of paper to prioritize the order in which you will be paying off these debts. Create seven columns across the top of your page. In this example we will be using a DEF number of $1,000. Your DEF may be more or less.

Steps

Step 1 – Column one, write the name of each creditor down the page.

Step 2 – Fill in the total balances due for each creditor in column 2. Then bring the totals down.

Step 3 – Fill in your monthly minimum payment in column 3.

Step 4 – Divide the total balance owed from your creditors by the monthly payment and place it in column 4 for each debt.

Step 5 – Now, take the lowest division answer and place a number 1 next to it in column 5.   Continue with the next highest division answer and mark it as number 2. Continue prioritizing the remaining creditors in column 5 until all are completed.   If any of your answers where of the same value, take the debt with the lowest amount and put it in as the next debt in order of priority.

Step 6 – In column 6, take the priority debt 1 and add your DEF to the monthly payment amount. Now place that amount into column 6.

Step 7 – Now divide debt 1's total balance by the new DEF amount and place the number into column 7. The answer is the number of months until this debt is completely paid off.

Step 8 – Once debt 1 is paid in full, take the minimum monthly payment + DEF and now add this amount to debt 2's monthly payment. This total will now be the monthly amount to pay on debt 2 until it is paid in full. Be sure to only pay the minimum monthly payment on all other debts.

Step 9 – Now continue adding each of the paid off debts DEF to the monthly payments of each of the next priority debts until you've completed each of your debts.

You're now **DEBT FREE!** And ready to start building wealth!

Tips to Remember

1. Prioritize each debt following the above directions.

2. Take all of your DEF and add it to the first debt's monthly payment. You will be focusing all your efforts on one debt at a time. Continue to pay that amount each month until that debt is eliminated.

3. Remember to stay focused on only one debt at a time and pay only the minimum payment on all other debts.

4. Once the first bill is eliminated, simply apply the DEF + the minimum payment from the first debt and apply them to the next debt's minimum payment amount. Each bill that you

eliminate will increase your DEF to be applied to the next debt in ranking order until you are debt free.

5.   The program is very easy to implement, it will just take commitment and action for it to work for you. Commit today that you will follow the easy steps to reach your new debt free life.

6.   Consider stopping any investing activities and apply all your investment dollars towards your DEF. By doing this you can eliminate your debt even faster. Later in the book I'll show you how important it is to only focus on eliminating debt. It can actually help you wind up with more money and wealth in the long term. It is not

recommended to work on reducing debts and investing at the same time. When paying down debts, every payment you make returns an actual rate of return equal to the interest rate of that debt. If you are being charged 22% interest and pay down or pay off that debt you have received a 22% rate of return on the money paid on that debt. You are now reversing what the debtors are doing to you. You are using reverse compounding in your favor instead of having compounding interest used against you.

7.   Having compounding interest work in your favor is what we're after. It is compounding interest being used in the reverse in your current situation that

will help you eliminate your debts in the quickest way.

8.   Staying focused and taking continual action towards your debts could be one of the most important factors for your success.

9.   With the economy tanking, job loss at an all-time high, and gas prices increasing, the time to take action is now.   Remember your retirement future stands on your shoulders alone. Take a look at where you are today and then focus on where you want to be in the future. It has been said that insanity is defined as doing the same thing over and over and expecting a different result. We have to change for success to happen.

10. You can use debt elimination software such as http://debt.bizcalcs.com to calculate your estimated debt free date.

The Quickest Path to Wealth

"The people who get on in this world are the people who get up and look for the circumstances they want, and if they can't find them, make them."
George Bernard Shaw

The quickest way to real wealth is to work on eliminating your debt the fastest way possible. The fastest way possible to eliminate debt is to focus all your extra income or DEF and apply it to your debts first and foremost.

Once your debts are eliminated you can focus all your income minus expenses towards accumulating wealth and do it faster than someone trying to eliminate debt and save for the future at the same time.

By using the Debt Elimination software (http://debt.bizcalcs.com) you will have the approximate amount of years until you are debt free.

When you're debt-free you'll be able to use all the DEF money, which has been accumulating as each debt is paid off and is now a sizable amount of money.

When those debts are paid off you can quickly accumulate a large sum of money in a short amount of time.

Let's take a look at two individuals in similar situations but each took different paths in eliminating their debts to build wealth.

Let's assume Tom and Bob are both debt-free with the exception of their mortgages. Tom and Bob both own homes with mortgage loans totaling $120,000 each with a 6% interest rate on 30-year loans. Both men pay a monthly mortgage payment of $844.

Tom is going to dedicate his DEF of $2,035 + $844, the amount of his mortgage payment, to paying off his mortgage. That's a total of $2,879 going toward his mortgage. Bob, on the other hand will continue to only pay his monthly mortgage payment of $844.

If Bob continues to pay his monthly payment of $844 until the mortgage is paid in full he will have paid $132,055 in interest payments alone and $252,055 in total payments over the course of this 30-year lone.

Tom on the other hand was able to repay his home in about 6 years by using his DEF and monthly mortgage payment amount combined.

Tom will have saved $65,084 in interest payments alone.

Additionally, Tom will have paid his mortgage off approximately twenty four years earlier than Bob. If Tom continued to invest the full DEF + his monthly mortgage payment of $2,879 over those twenty four years and earned an average rate of return of 10% Tom would now have approximately $3,773,494.55 in savings.

The calculations for the above example were conducted by using bankrate.com's simple savings calculator.

This example, my friends is using compounding interest to your advantage and shows that paying off debt first and not mixing debt reduction with investing can provide you with great wealth.

Debt elimination is one of the most important steps in achieving true wealth.

There are investment guru's that will lead you to believe you should save for an emergency fund before attempting to eliminate your debts. I disagree with that principle if you're looking for the fastest way to become debt-free.

If a true emergency arises you have one credit card you kept open for that situation. You also should have a sizable DEF amount each month. If a debt arises you can use the DEF amount which should cover most of the emergencies unless it is a sizable amount.

If you need to use your DEF for an emergency it will delay your originally planned debt payoff date a month while providing the needed money for the emergency.

Let's take another look at Tom and Bob in a different situation. Tom and Bob have debt and Tom is going to reduce his debt and rely on his credit card and DEF if any emergencies arise while paying down and eliminating his debt.

Bob on the other hand feels the need to save in an emergency fund. Bob listens to the so called experts who recommend saving six months of living expenses.

Tom and Bob have the same expenses of $2,879 each month. Bob starts saving in his emergency fund but can only apply $350 of the $2,879 due to his living expenses.

It will take Bob four years and one month to fund his emergency fund. Once he has accomplished saving enough to have a fully funded emergency fund he will now start the debt elimination program.

It will take Bob another four years to become debt-free.

Tom is going to use his DEF to pay off his debts first. Tom will pay off his debts in five years and one month. Now that Tom has paid off his debts his monthly living expenses have reduced to approximately $975.

If Tom continues to use his DEF it should only take him around two months to fund his emergency fund.

After funding his emergency fund which only took two months Tom starts using his DEF to open and fund an investment account.

Tom will have paid off his debts and fully funded his emergency fund two years and ten months earlier than Bob.

If Tom continued to fund his investment account over the span of those two years and ten months with the $2,879, Tom would have built his investment fund to approximately $97,886 not including any interest.

I hope you are starting to see that by increasing your DEF and applying it to your debts you will definitely get out of debt quicker than someone trying to reduce their debts and trying to pay themselves a small amount of money.

You only have so much DEF to use each month and when you try to put a small amount of money into too many different locations it lessens the effectiveness of what your money could be doing for you.

It is a much better idea to put all your DEF into one place and annihilate that debt. Every time you pay off another debt your DEF builds. Every time another debt is paid off it will also lower your living expenses. Compounding in this manner is what helps you accomplish your goal of becoming debt-free in such a small amount of time compared to the average household.

Credit Card Company's use compounding against you buy offering such low minimum monthly payments. The low monthly payments and high interest rates is what keep you in debt for years.

To reduce the effects of that compounding we are making a large DEF payment which quickly reduces the high interest rates affect and eliminates the debts very quickly.

"The most powerful force in the world is compounding interest."

Albert Einstein

If You Believe It, You Can Achieve It

"Make a decision to be successful right now. Most people never decide to be wealthy and that is why they retire poor."
Brian Tracy

The above examples and numbers used should make it easier to see that you can achieve a debt-free lifestyle, and most of you can achieve that goal within a relatively short time.

Once we let our minds believe that we can be debt free in a short time, our minds can start working toward the goal.

If you believe it you can achieve is a simple statement at face value. When you apply this simple statement to your life it will help to reassure you that when you follow these simple techniques you can achieve a lifelong dream in a short amount of time.

I know some may say, "Yah, it's still going to take me 5, 6, 7, years to become debt free." I'd compare that to the 90%+ of the individuals that never achieve a debt-free life. Yes, it is going to take focus, determination and a will to change the way you currently look at money.

I would ask those people this question? "Where will you be in five years if you don't apply these techniques to eliminate your debt in five years?" They would probably need to answer yes, for in five years they will still be in debt and probably have even more debt.

No matter how you look at it, you are going to have to take responsibility for where you are, decide to change your financial future, and eliminate debt.

It may take you a few years to eliminate your debts but what is your plan if you don't accept the amount of years it may take you to get out of debt.

Either way you look at it, at some point you are going to have to reduce your debt or retire as one of the 90% statistics.

The debt won't go away by itself and the sooner you address the debt, the more money you could possibly have at retirement age.

Don't be an Ostrich and bury your head in the sand hoping your debt will go away. Those debts will still be there when you come up for air, even if it's as late as the day you decide to retire.

The techniques I've provided for you within this book will help you to a debt free life in the shortest amount of time possible.

Take a second of your time and remember back five years ago. It doesn't really seem that long ago does it. I can remember back twenty one years ago when I graduated college and it sometimes seems like yesterday.

I just want to help you succeed at achieving your goals. In my opinion it is a shame to see so many people working their entire lives and retiring broke or in debt with little or no money in the bank.

I truly would like to help any individuals and families turn those statistics around. I know my age group cannot start drawing social security until age 79. Some companies have taken away pensions and implemented a 401K match.

It appears to me that we are going to have to fund our retirement ourselves and that is going to require that we learn how to reduce our debts and build wealth ourselves if we want any shot of having a financially independent lifestyle by the time we retire.

"A penny saved is a penny earned."
Ben Franklin

"The great successful men of the world have used their imagination, they think ahead and create their mental picture in all its details, filling in here, adding a little there, altering this a bit and that a bit, but steadily building – steadily building."
Robert Collier

Dream Big

"Part of your heritage in this society is the opportunity to become financially independent."
Jim Rohn

Now that you have your plan in place and are starting to reduce your debt you can start dreaming about the lifestyle you will be able to afford in a only a few short years.

With all your bills paid off you can lead a stress free life. You won't have to worry if your company downsizes and you're laid off. You have no debt and could quickly find another job to pay for your small monthly expenses.

Take some time to think what you will do when you achieve your goals, what will your ideal day look like. Will you take that lifetime dream vacation with your spouse or significant other, or will you take up golfing and hit the links every morning after breakfast?

If you now see that a debt-free lifestyle is imminent and you can now see your dreams becoming a reality, it will help you to stay focused and motivated at the same time.

"People with goals succeed because they know where they're going."
Earl Nightingale

Dream Board

"The difference between a successful person and others is not a lack of strength, not a lack of knowledge, but rather in a lack of will."
Vincent T. Lombardi

You may even enjoy creating a dream board. Get a cork board and start cutting pictures of the home you want to retire in and place it on the board. Clip pictures of the cars you want to drive, maybe the cruise you want to go on, or the tropical vacation with the beautiful view of crystal clear water and while you're sitting in your hammock, you can see the beach close by.

Keep your visual board in a location where you can see it every day. It can help you stay motivated and focused on achieving your new goals.

When you allow your mind to see the lifestyle you desire and keep implementing the debt reduction techniques, you will be reminded every day of how important it is to take continued action until you achieve your goal.

I think it is important to create some sort of visualization for the things you want in life. If you have a roadmap you can reach any location by the quickest, most direct route. A vision board can be your roadmap.

It shows you every day where you want to go, and by applying the techniques in this book you'll have the vehicle to get you to your destination. If you can't see where you want to go, you could take a wrong turn, which would take you longer to get to your destination.

Keeping the dream board before your eyes every day can help you stay focused and on the correct path to arrive at your destination on time.

"Goals in writing are dreams with deadlines."
Brian Tracy

Things to Think About

"It is our attitude at the beginning of a difficult task which, more than anything else, will affect its successful outcome."
William James

If you don't start today, when will you start a financial plan for success?

Can you afford not to change your financial future?

Are you going to retire in debt, or choose to be financially free?

Do you have financial goals, or a roadmap to get where you want to go?

Are you and your love ones more important than purchasing yourself into a whole lot of debt?

Saying no to your loved ones unnecessary purchases do not mean you don't love them.

Are you determined to do whatever it takes to eliminate your debt and retire financially free?

If you are not going to fund your retirement, who is? Do you know with an easier plan to eliminate debt that won't require budgeting?

Where will you be in ten years from now if you don't start your financial plan today?

Remember, if you start today you could be out of debt within a handful of years.

Is this not one of the most important decisions of your life that you will ever have to make?

When following this program, I want to assure you this is not a program of scarcity. You are in control of your financial future.

I'm just suggesting you rethink what caused your debt while providing you with way's to conquer your debt once and for all.

I would like to think of this program as an educational look into why you are in debt; providing you with the necessary tools to get you out of debt, so you can build wealth.

You are ultimately in control of where you wind up. Try and live below your means, but taking care of your needs. By delaying or putting a stop to impulse buying, and not yielding to low, easily affordable payment options, you are stopping future debt from occurring. You are taking back your financial future, one step at a time.

When thinking about purchasing an item don't fall for old marketing tricks; They may tell you there are limited quantities, and you must order now before the commercial ends. If you act now we'll throw in one more for free! Order now!!! Don't fall for these debt traps.

I'm not saying you shouldn't buy those items you need, but you must take control of your purchasing decisions and not allow others to take your money while the credit card company spends more of your future earnings, plus interest.

You could write down the number from the ad, then take a break from the television, and do something else, delay gratification for a short time.

Think through the purchasing decision after some time has passed. Do you still feel the same? Do you still want to make that purchase?

If you allow some time to go by it's like a cooling off period that will keep you from getting sucked into their excellent marketing tactics.

I know when I do this technique, I'm less likely to still want what I thought I couldn't live without, and I am more level-headed about the decision to purchase.

You learned the importance of not using credit cards, closing the accounts with exception of one for emergencies only. You are empowering yourself to become your own bank, not leaning on the expensive crutch of credit that will cost your future investment dollars.

Spend some time creating financial goals; post them where you see and read them daily.

Create a dream board so you can see where you want to go. When you can see where you want to be, and you look at your chosen images every day, you will begin to believe the dream is coming true and it will give you strength to finish your debt elimination program.

I know you can do this and all it takes is determination, action and sticking with the plan for a handful of years to achieve the lifestyle you truly desire.

I implore you to take action today, follow a plan of action to secure your financial success. If you don't do it, who will? You have all you need to change your financial destiny.

There are really only two choices here, join the statistic of retiring in debt and stress or join the statistic that owns their lives and is financially free to do the things they want to do.

No matter what obstacle stands in your way, you must choose to overcome it and stay the course. It may not always be easy but if you don't overcome those obstacles now, where will you wind up? Choose to be a success; you'll be glad you did.

"I shall find a way or make one."
Robert Edwin Peary

Special Thank You

"Success doesn't come to you, you go to it."

Marva Collins

I want to thank you for purchasing this book. I take your financial future seriously and I know you will too now that you've read this book. It is truly my desire to see you become debt-free and begin building wealth.

I have been in your shoes and know the stress it caused for me and my family.

I'm sure if you apply the techniques in this book you will achieve your goals too.

When I started on my debt elimination journey I had a hard time finding the money I needed to apply to my DEF.

I started researching how I could locate more money that was leaking out of my life so I could fill those holes. I took those savings and applied them to my debts to reduce the time it would take to eliminate my debts.

In my book **"101 Money Saving Tips to Help Reduce Debt and Build Wealth (Financial Prosperity Series),"** I reveal the top 101 tips I used to increase my monthly DEF.

If you are having problems finding enough money for your DEF or you would like to increase your DEF, you may consider picking up a copy of my book, click on the above link or copy and paste the book title into the Amazon.com search bar.

You now have everything you need to achieve your goals of a debt-free lifestyle.

Once you're debt-free you'll have a nice sized DEF that you can then invest to build your wealth.

The sooner you start the program, the sooner you will achieve your goal. Every day you prolong implementing a debt reduction program that is one more day you are costing yourself future investment dollars that you could have toward creating the wealth you deserve.

I wish you all the best in your debt reduction and building wealth goals. I have faith in your ability to make your dreams come true. Stay focused, determined and Crush those debts!

"At least eighty percent of millionaires are self-made. That is, they started with nothing but ambition and energy, the same way most of us start."

      Brian Tracy

Wishing You All the Best,

J. P. Conyers, Jr.

www.ingramcontent.com/pod-product-compliance
Lightning Source LLC
Chambersburg PA
CBHW072024190526
45166CB00015B/468